WEST CHICAGO ~~~~

D0991679

4/04

$4.45

West Chicago Public Library District
118 West Washington
West Chicago, IL 60185-2803
Phone # (630) 231-1552

Land and Resources of Ancient Rome

Daniel C. Gedacht

The Rosen Publishing Group's
PowerKids Press™
PRIMARY SOURCE

New York

For my wife, Eti. Thank you for everything.

Published in 2004 by The Rosen Publishing Group, Inc.
29 East 21st Street, New York, NY 10010

Copyright © 2004 by The Rosen Publishing Group, Inc.

All rights reserved. No part of this book may be reproduced in any form without permission in writing from the publisher, except by a reviewer.

First Edition

Editor: Rachel O'Connor
Designer: Michael J. Caroleo
Photo Researcher: Adriana Skura

Photo Credits: Cover The Art Archive/Archeological Museum Cherchel Algeria/Dagli Orti; cover (inset) and p. 11 (left) © Erich Lessing/Art Resource, NY; p. 4 © Dennis Degnan/CORBIS; pp. 4 (inset), 12 (inset), 19 (inset) © Hulton/Archive/Getty Images; p. 7 © Michael Maslan Historic Photographs/CORBIS; p. 8 (left) The Art Archive; p. 8 (right) The Art Archive/Real Collegiata San Isidoro Leon/Dagli Orti; p. 11 (top) The Art Archive/Museo del Sannio Benevento/Dagli Orti; p. 11 (right) The Art Archive/Palazzo Barberini Rome/Dagli Orti; p. 12 © Corinne Humphrey/Index Stock Imagery, Inc; p. 15 © Dennis Marsico/CORBIS; pp. 16, 19 The Art Archive/Dagli Orti; p. 20 © Dallas and John Heaton/CORBIS, (inset) © Vanni Archives/CORBIS.

Gedacht, Daniel C.
  Land and resources of ancient Rome / Daniel C. Gedacht.
    p. cm. — (Primary sources of ancient civilizations. Rome)   Includes bibliographical references and index.
  Contents: The Roman Empire—The Mediterranean Sea—Geography and climate—Ancient Roman agriculture—Natural defenses—Roman rivers—Building resources—What the Romans built—Aqueducts—From city to empire.
  ISBN 0-8239-6775-1 (library binding) — ISBN 0-8239-8943-7 (pbk.)
  1. Rome—Civilization—Juvenile literature. 2. Rome—Geography—Juvenile literature. 3. Natural resources—Rome—Juvenile literature. [1. Rome—Civilization. 2. Rome—Geography. 3. Natural resources—Rome.] I. Title. II. Series.
  DG78.G39 2004
  937—dc21   2002154177
Manufactured in the United States of America

Contents

The Roman Empire

In ancient times, Rome was much more than a city in Italy. It was an empire. It began as a city in the eighth century B.C. However, by 27 B.C., the ancient Romans had conquered all of what is now Italy, southern Europe, North Africa, and the Middle East.

The land and resources of Italy were important to the Roman Empire. Rome's large areas of fertile land allowed the ancient Romans to grow much of the food that they needed. Any foods or other resources they could not produce themselves, the ancient Romans imported from the countries they had conquered. The land also offered valuable resources such as limestone and marble.

◀ *Italy's land was fertile and rich in natural resources. This photograph shows the countryside in central Italy. Inset: The Pantheon was a temple built by the Romans, using such natural resources as marble, to honor their gods.*

The Mediterranean Sea

   Italy is a peninsula in south-central Europe. Rome is located on Italy's western shore, which borders the Mediterranean Sea. The Mediterranean was an important resource to the growth of the Roman Empire. To gain complete access to all of this sea's trade routes, the ancient Romans set out to conquer the countries that bordered the Mediterranean. They succeeded in conquering countries such as Greece, Egypt, and Spain. This access allowed the Romans to ship their armies to territories that they wanted to attack. The Roman Empire's location on the Mediterranean Sea was important to Rome's keeping its political, economic, and military power.

This map of Italy shows the Italian peninsula, bordered by water on three sides. The Tyrrhenian Sea, which is part of the Mediterranean, is to the west, the Ionian Sea is to the south, and the Adriatic Sea is to the east. ▶

Adriatic Sea

Tyrrhenian Sea

Mediterranean Sea

Ionian Sea

7

AGUSTVS

8

Geography and Climate

Italy's geography is a mixture of mountains, plains, and hills. Much of the land is fertile and suitable for farming. Ancient Roman farmers grew wheat and corn, among other crops, on the land. One of the most fertile regions in Italy is the Po River valley, where most of Italy's flat land is located. The Po valley is in northern Italy, where the climate is moderate.

Farther south, Italy has a Mediterranean climate. This climate typically has mild, wet winters and hot, dry summers. The ancient Romans found that grapes and olives grew well in such weather on the hilly land in southern Italy.

Left: *The September grape harvest is shown in this stone carving from Baptistery at Paema, Italy.* Right: *This fresco shows Roman agriculture during the summer months.*

Ancient Roman Agriculture

The Romans were able to enjoy plentiful harvests because of the fertile land and the varied climate. The ancient Romans believed that, if they prayed to Ceres, the Roman goddess of agriculture, she would help their harvests. They also had developed expert farming techniques.

The Romans grew vegetables and made olive oil from the olives that grew in Italy. As the Romans conquered new territories, they were able to add to their natural resources. For example, the Romans ate grains such as barley and wheat, which was used to make bread. Much of the grain came from parts of North Africa, which the Romans had conquered.

Top: Ancient Romans used oxen to plow their fields, as shown in this second-century marble sculpture. Right: Ceres was the goddess of ▶ agriculture. Inset: This mosaic shows a baker putting bread into an oven.

11

Natural Defenses

The Alps, located on the northern border of Italy, separated Italy from the rest of Europe. During the winter, the Alps provided the ancient Romans with a natural defense boundary. The cold and the snow made the Alps hard to cross. During the summer, however, the Alps were accessible to invaders. The Apennines, a mountain range that runs through the center of Italy, also provided some protection. The sea acted as a natural barrier before Rome's enemies built ships.

Although Italy possessed some barriers, the land could not always provide protection. To defend themselves from frequent attacks, the ancient Romans had to develop their fighting skills.

◄ *This is an aerial view of the Italian Alps. Inset: The Romans became a powerful military force partly because of insufficient natural barriers. This image shows Roman military ships during the Roman war with Carthage.*

Roman Rivers

The main rivers in Italy are the Po in the north, the Adige in the northeast, and the Tiber, which flows south through central Italy. Rivers were a very important natural resource in ancient Rome. They irrigated the surrounding farmlands, provided fresh water, and were used for trade and transport.

The ancient city of Rome grew around the banks of the Tiber River. As the city developed, the Tiber provided the ancient Romans with fresh water for their everyday living requirements. Boats sailed on the Tiber carrying goods or soldiers from Rome to the Mediterranean Sea and beyond.

This is a modern-day view of the Tiber River, which flows through Rome. In the background is St. Peter's Basilica, a cathedral that was built ▶
between 1506 and 1626.

16

Building Resources

The Romans used the natural resources available to them, such as limestone and volcanic ash, for building materials. There were many active volcanoes on the west coast of Italy that provided the Romans with ash. They made concrete by mixing volcanic ash, limestone powder, and water. They roasted the limestone, which came from the soil, until it turned into powder. Roman buildings had strong supports such as columns and arches made of concrete. The Romans imported resources they did not have from territories they had conquered. One reason the Romans conquered Britain was to gain access to its mines of lead and tin, which they used in building.

◀ *Natural resources such as stone and cement were used to build great buildings such as the Colosseum, the remains of which can be seen here. The Colosseum was a large space where sporting events were held.*

17

What the Romans Built

Defending their empire was very important to the ancient Romans. They built huge walls, about 9 feet (2.7 m) thick, to protect their towns. They usually built these walls with bricks. Bricks were made from mud that had dried and hardened in the sun.

The Romans built roads for trade and military transport. They built about 50,000 miles (80,467.2 km) of roads using their natural resources, stone and concrete. The first major road was built in 312 B.C. It was called the Via Appia, or Appian Way, and is still used today. They also built temples and theaters, which they decorated with the marble they mined in quarries in Italy.

The Appian Way is one example of the roads the Romans built. ▶
Inset: *This second-century drawing shows the plan of the Pantheon.*

Elevation and Plan of the Colosseum

19

Aqueducts

The rivers in Italy provided the ancient Romans with fresh water. They used the water for drinking, cooking, and washing, and for irrigating the land. River water needed to be harnessed, however. Once the empire expanded and the population began to grow, the ancient Romans built aqueducts and sewers to bring freshwater to the cities and towns that were far away from the rivers. Aqueducts were arched waterways that were built of stone and concrete. Lead pipes brought water from the reservoir into the city, and drains and sewers took the used and dirty water away. The ancient Romans imported lead from their British territory.

◀ *This modern-day photo shows the Pont du Gard aqueduct, built by the Romans, in Nimes, France.* Top: *The lead pipes that the Romans used in their irrigation systems were later found to be harmful to peoples' health.*

From City to Empire

Rome was one of ancient civilization's most important centers for trade and commerce, partly because of its resources. It was situated on the Tiber, so it had access to the Mediterranean. The thousands of miles (km) of roads that the Romans built helped them to maintain growth in commerce. The ancient Romans built a great military force because their land did not offer them enough protection. Their empire was able to flourish because of the huge amounts of food they could grow and the products they were able to make. The land and resources of ancient Rome helped it to develop from a small city on the Tiber River into one of the greatest and most powerful empires in history.

Glossary

access (AK-ses) A way to get somewhere easily.

aerial (EHR-ee-ul) Of or in the air.

commerce (KAH-mers) Buying or selling goods on a large scale, which involves shipping them from place to place.

defense (dih-FENS) Saving from harm.

develop (dih-VEH-lup) To grow.

expanded (ek-SPAND-ed) Spread out, or grew larger.

expert (EK-spert) Having to do with knowing a lot about a subject.

fertile (FER-tul) Good for making and growing things.

imported (im-PORT-ed) Brought from another country for sale or use.

invaders (in-VAYD-erz) People who enter a place in order to attack and take over.

irrigated (EER-ih-gayt-ed) Supplied land with water through ditches or pipes.

materials (muh-TEER-ee-ulz) What something is made of.

peninsula (peh-NIN-suh-luh) An area of land surrounded by water on three sides.

quarries (KWOR-eez) Large holes, dug in the ground, from which stone is taken.

reservoir (REH-zuh-vwar) A stored body of water.

resources (REE-sors-es) Supplies or sources of energy or useful materials.

transport (TRANZ-port) The act of moving something from one place to another.

Index

Primary Sources

Cover. This mosaic, circa A.D. 100–200, shows Romans working in the fields with oxen. From the Dagli Orti collection in the Archaeological Museum, Cherchel, Algeria. **Inset.** This is a stone sculpture showing men transporting wine barrels by ship. The stone relief is circa A.D. 100–300. **Page 4.** A modern-day view of the countryside in Val d'Orcia, Tuscany, Italy. Photograph by Dennis Degnan. Circa 2002. **Page 11. Top.** This marble relief is from the second century A.D. It is a depiction of ancient Romans ploughing and harvesting their crops. From the Dagli Orti collection in the Muswo del Sannio Benevento. **Bottom.** A baker is shown here putting bread into an oven. This mosaic is circa A.D.100–300. It is from a series that shows agricultural work year-round in Saint Romain-en-Gal, France. **Page 15.** Tiber River at the Arch Bridge in Rome. Photograph by Dennis Marsico. 1995. **Page 20.** View of the Pont du Gard. Photograph by Dallas and John Heaton. The three-tiered aqueduct spans over Gard River and the green valley, running from Uzes to Nimes, France. **Inset.** Roman aqueduct lead piping. Photograph by Ruggero Vanni. If an aqueduct provided water to Rome, it carried the name of the emperor who was ruling at the time it was built. On the lead pipes shown here, we can read, "Aureli Cesaris," for Marcus Aurelius.

Web Sites

Due to the changing nature of Internet links, PowerKids Press has developed an online list of Web sites related to the subject of this book. This site is updated regularly. Please use this link to access the list:

www.powerkidslinks.com/psaciv/landrom/